The Bedside Book of Railway History

60p

The Bedside Book
of Railway History

by

R. O. T. Povey

Dalesman Books
1974

The Dalesman Publishing Company Ltd.,
Clapham (via Lancaster), Yorkshire
First published 1974
© R. O. T. Povey, 1974.

ISBN: 0 85206 221 4

Printed and bound in Great Britain by
FRETWELL & BRIAN LTD.
Silsden, Nr. Keighley, Yorkshire.

Contents

Front cover painting by Ionicus. Back cover photographs show:-
Top: The Northern Dales Railtour crossing Stainmore viaduct on the Darlington - Penrith line in 1955; Bottom: A "Deltic" diesel at Riccarton Junction on a "last train" over the Waverley Route in 1969. The title page drawing is of George Stephenson's birthplace at Wylam, Northumberland.

Photographs supplied by British Railways, G. G. Hoare, David Joy and L & GRP. All maps and drawings by the author.

Introduction

I HAVE never wanted to be an engine driver. Many of my contemporaries expressed a desire to make this their life's work but they all settled down as accountants or civil servants or something equally unexciting. This is not to say, however, that railways have not held other facinations for me. My first home was on the very lineside of the London and North Western main line from Chester to Manchester and it was at a gradient summit at that. I am sure I felt that Mr. Webb and Mr. Bowen-Cooke had designed the sound-effects as well as the engines and all this for my personal delight.

When we lived at that house, we had only two fields to cross to reach the Cheshire Lines Railway, but the teak coaches seemed quite uninteresting by comparison with the L.N.W.R. livery and the engines were disgustingly capable of dealing with any train without the sound-effects. No, the L. N.W.R. was a real working railway.

About 1930 we moved house to within a couple of hundred yards of the Great Western Railway and, after a little while, my loyalties changed. Here we had freight yards and sidings all around and in those days there was much activity with the little pannier tank shunters. Loose shunting went on all night and I do not think I could have got off to sleep without this lullaby. The main line to the North Wales coast was also quite near and to take up a position near Saltney Junction signal box was to see all sorts of engines and trains passing at intervals of but a few minutes.

But still I didn't want to become an engine driver. When my interest later turned towards social history, I found that the railways played a large part in developing man's attitude to his environment and I felt that what really interested me about railways was their history.

In the course of my readings I have come across a number of amusing or interesting pieces of information and, believing that they would amuse or interest others, I have set them down and offer them to you now in the form of a "Bedside Book of Railway History".

R.O.T.P.

Southern England

Pardon!

ON THE 29th October 1838 four broad gauge carriages of the Great Western Railway were standing on the line at Maidenhead and were set in motion by the wind. Two of the carriages were halted at Slough while the other two continued for a distance of 20 miles to Wormwood Scrubs.

Carry Your Bag, Sir?

THE Liskeard and Caradon Railway was built as a freight line and was never authorised to carry passengers. This difficulty was overcome by carrying passengers free at their own risk and making a charge for the carriage of their personal freight (hats, handbags, etc.).

A Bad Beginning

AT THE official opening of the Bristol and Gloucester Railway on the 8th July 1844 a train laden with honoured guests and officials was approaching Gloucester when the rails spread, causing the engine and several carriages to drop on to the ballast. No one was injured so the passengers disembarked and walked to their destination.

Gauges, Broad and Narrow

THE Exeter and Crediton Railway obtained an Act of Parliament in 1845 to build a six-mile line from a junction with the Bristol and Exeter Railway which under the Act was to work the new route. Both lines were on the broad gauge (7ft 0¼ins. between the rails).

It so happened that the London and South Western Railway saw in this line a useful addition to its own empire which was, incidentally, on the narrow (4ft 8½ins) gauge. In order to try to bring its influence to bear on the E. & C., the L. & S. W. bought up what shares it could in this little railway until about two years later it felt that something could be done.

The Taw Valley Railway was then induced to propose to the Exeter and Crediton that the line should be leased to the Taw Valley and that the lease should be guaranteed by the L. & S. W. This came as a shock to the local shareholders who remained loyal to the idea of the line being worked by the Bristol and Exeter. A meeting was held to consider the proposal but, agreement not being reached, the shareholders had to be called together again at a later date.

Between these meetings the directors tried to get the line open as it was virtually complete. However, the Taw Valley Company obtained an injunction to stop the line being opened with a connection to the Bristol and Exeter until its proposition of a lease had been considered. The resumed meeting was on the 12th April 1847 and various devices were used by the "invading party". They proposed to sack some of the original directors; they disputed the authority of the chairman and generally caused uproar in the meeting.

This broad gauge line now stood ready for immediate use but in view of the injunction it lay unused for over a year. At the end of this time, the narrow gauge champions had sufficient control to be able to order the ripping out of the broad gauge track and the substitution of narrow gauge. There was thus a narrow gauge line standing in the middle of nowhere with a connection to a broad gauge line at a point outside Exeter.

It was then proposed that the Exeter and Crediton might be extended as a narrow gauge line by its own route right into Exeter but as the amount of capital authorised by the Act of Parliament had already been spent this was not possible. The narrow gauge party tried, nevertheless, to get the line opened but the Railway Commissioners pointed out that the Act authorised a broad gauge line and it should not on any account be opened on the narrow gauge. This put a stop to the whole business and the line lay unused for some years longer.

Eventually another Act was obtained to allow for further capital to be raised whereupon the Exeter and Crediton was relaid as a broad gauge line and opened on the 12th May 1851 to be worked by the Bristol and Exeter—all as originally planned. In the later years (1862) the line was taken into the London and South Western and re-converted to the 4' 8½" gauge as part of the North Devon line.

Escape Route

THE railway navvies learned a number of special skills in the course of their work and in 1846, when one of these men was locked up in the town gaol at Swindon, his mates tunnelled under the floor and let him out.

The Case For A Broad Gauge Throat

ISAMBARD Kingdom Brunel, engineer to the Great Western Railway, was once entertaining children at a party with a few conjuring tricks, for which he was well-known, when he accidentally swallowed a half-sovereign. To be more precise, he *inhaled* it, for it lodged in his windpipe.

Surgery was not then in the state of perfection in which we are used to finding it today and an operation attempted by Sir Benjamin Brodie proved to be unsuccessful. Not to be easily defeated Mr. Brunel applied his fertile mind to the invention of a special contrivance which whirled him round at a tremendous speed. The centrifugal force thus created expelled the half-sovereign which had been fixed in his throat for no less than six weeks.

9

Not You, Dick

ON THE Cornwall Railway in 1873 signalling was still done verbally at the single line passing places, and on one occasion at Menheniot an up and a down goods train were awaiting dispatch. By coincidence both guards rejoiced in the Christian name of Richard. On getting the "Right away, Dick" the wrong man set off with the result that his train met an express coming in the opposite direction.

Thick Twist

ON THE conversion of the Great Western Railway to standard gauge in May 1892, Mr. Wills of the firm of W.D. & H.O. Wills presented five thousand two-ounce packets of "Westward Ho!" twist for the use of the men engaged on the work. It is estimated that the gift cost Mr. Wills, who was also a director of the G.W.R., £150.

An Englishman's Car Is His "Castle"

G. J. CHURCHWARD of the Great Western Railway built himself a steam motor car to go about in.

Twice Bitten

ON THE 4th March 1839 a driver on the London and Southampton Railway gave two young ladies an unauthorised footplate trip. Punishments were hard in those days and the company fined him £2. Shortly afterwards the same driver helped a passenger to avoid paying his fare by giving him a ride in the tender. This was too much for the directors who dismissed the driver.

Red For Danger

ON THE 29th July 1845 a train arrived at Tonbridge from Dover and detached the rear coach. It was dark and the person responsible for the uncoupling forgot to change the tail light forward to the next carriage. When the train had got away he remembered this omission and set off in pursuit on a light engine. Unfortunately the driver of the light engine ran into the back of the train he was chasing because it had no tail light!

Thirty people were injured and two coaches smashed.

Biter Bit?

BETWEEN Falmer and Lewes on the London, Brighton and South Coast Railway on the 6th June 1851, five persons lost their lives when a down passenger train left the rails suddenly and, running across the up line, plunged 25 feet down on to the road.

It was thought that a boy had deliberately placed a sleeper across one rail but the case was not proved against him. Strange to relate, the boy was killed while trespassing on the line at about the same place on the same date of the following year.

Self Punishment

ON THE 27th November 1851 near Ford station on the London, Brighton and South Coast Railway a passenger train collided with a cattle train at a bridge over the river Arun. The driver of the cattle train jumped into the river to get clear of the accident, which had been caused by the driver of the passenger train missing his signals.

The driver of the passenger train attempted suicide on the spot by cutting his throat. As this did not work he, too, jumped into the river but was hauled out again by the guard.

Cows May Safely Graze

A HEAVY GOODS train of the London, Brighton and South Coast Railway was being taken up a gradient of 1 in 80 between Lewes and Falmer on 3rd October 1859, with the train engine at the front and a "banker" at the rear, when the boiler of the train engine burst through the firebox. The explosion threw the track out of alignment and gauge and the banker continued to push the leading wagons over the engine. The second wagon contained two cows which were thus elevated, but on being got down from their lofty perch they are reported to have grazed peacefully at the lineside.

A Fatal Decision

ON THE 5th June 1861 at Andover on the London and South Western Railway a driver discovered that he had lost part of his goods train and set back to look for the lost wagons. The stationmaster at Grateley had meantime found the wagons and, as the line was on a falling gradient, decided to work them forward by gravity. The two portions of the train collided, killing the stationmaster and injuring the brakesman.

Three into One Won't Go

THREE TRAINS of the London, Brighton and South Coast Railway due to leave Brighton for London at 8.5 a.m., 8.15 a.m., and 8.30 a.m. on the 25th August 1861, actually got away at 8.28, 8.31 and 8.35 respectively. The first one got through Clayton Tunnel but a treadle at the tunnel mouth, which should have automatically set a signal at danger, failed to operate and the driver of the following train assumed his road to be clear.

The signalman could clear the signal, after it had been set at danger and after receiving a telegraph clearance from the other end of the tunnel, but could not himself set it. On this occasion, therefore, he exhibited a red flag which the driver of the second train saw and acted upon, but could not stop his train until it was in the tunnel. He should then have stayed where he was and sent his guard back but instead he started to set back.

Meantime, the signalman, thinking the driver had not seen his signal, asked the signalman at the other end of the tunnel if the train had got right through. He thought this was a reference to the first train, not knowing that a second had entered the tunnel, and replied "yes". The result was that the third train was allowed into the tunnel unchecked and a collision ensued. Twenty-three persons were killed and 175 injured.

The Inspecting Officer, Capt. H. Tyler, pointed out that the time interval had not been adhered to and, in any case, recommended a space interval between trains as now known in the block system.

What The Dickens?

ON THE 9th June 1865 near Staplehurst, a gang were carrying out repairs to an underbridge. Some rails had been removed to facilitate the operation and, although a flagman had been posted and the weather was clear, the Creamers Patent Brake was unable to stop a passenger train before it dropped off the track.

Charles Dickens was among the passengers and it has been said that the shock of this accident hastened his death (which incidentally took place exactly five years later). The reason for the track being up when a train was due is said to be because the ganger mistook the day of the week.

Fantastic

ON THE 9th September 1873 a bullock strayed on to the London and South Western line near Guildford and was struck by an express train from Portsmouth. All the coaches were derailed but the engine and tender, breaking the coupling, leapt over the bullock, remained on the line and ran on to Guildford with the news. Three people were killed.

Drowning Of A Locomotive

THE Isle of Wight Railway had a new locomotive built by Beyer Peacock & Co. in 1883 and this was delivered from the mainland to St. Helens (Brading) Harbour. Unfortunately the locomotive—which was named *Bonchurch*—fell off the lighter which was bringing it ashore and it spent several days under salt water.

Taken For A Ride

TO CELEBRATE the opening of the Bideford Extension Railway, about 300 persons were allowed to travel free. Many of these intended not to return on the next train but to make a day of it and come back later in the evening. Much to their annoyance, the train which ran in the evening did not stop at the station at Bideford but halted a little way down the line to pick up some special passengers.

The stranded travellers had to manage as best they could to either get home to Fremington or sleep where they were. The local paper warned people to be careful of accepting free rides in the future.

Funeral Service

THE London Necropolis and National Mausoleum Company purchased 2,200 acres of land near Woking to provide a last refuge for deceased Londoners. A special railway was built to serve this huge cemetery and a special funeral train ran daily from Waterloo. Pauper corpses were charged 2s. 6d. (single, of course), working men 5s and the aristocracy 20s. Special rates also applied to the mourners up to a maximum of six persons per funeral; these, of course, were returns.

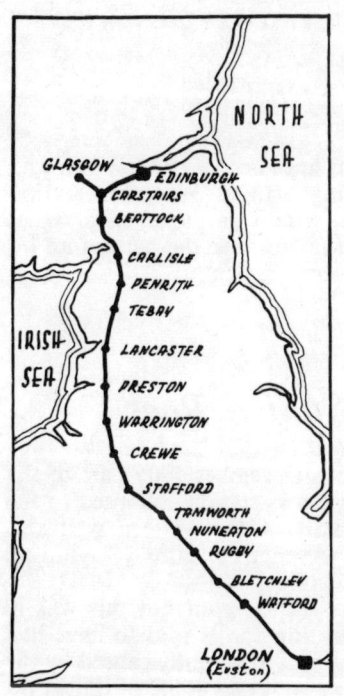

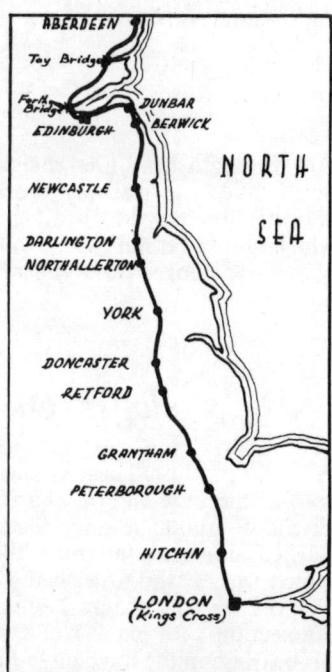

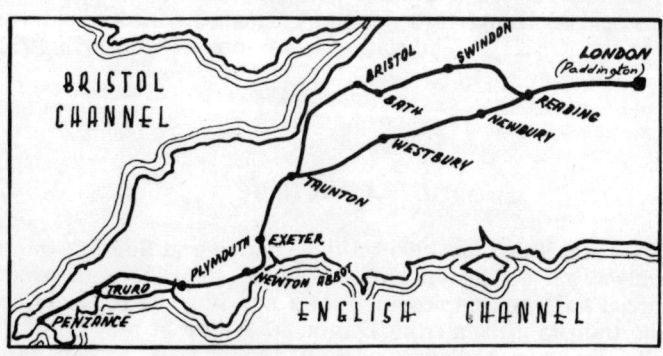

Main Lines out of London.

Spilt Milk

ON THE 5th May 1904 a signal linesman of the London and South Western Railway working around Waterloo station accidentally stepped on a signal wire. This pulled off a signal which allowed a milk train to draw out into the path of an incoming passenger train. There was one death.

Collapse Of Station Roof

AT 3.40 p.m. on Tuesday the 5th December 1905 part of the roof at the river end of Charing Cross station collapsed to the extent of about seventy feet. Part of the western wall was pushed out and fell into the Avenue Theatre (Playhouse) which was, at the time, being rebuilt.

Work was in progress on the station roof but this was in connection with glazing and painting and is said to have had no bearing on the incident, which was apparently caused by the failure of a tie-rod. Some railway staff and some of the workmen at the Avenue Theatre were killed and others injured. A Continental train was due in when the roof collapsed but was held on Hungerford Bridge by signals before it could run into the wreckage. The station was re-opened in March 1906.

Inexplicable

ON THE 30th June 1906 on the London and South Western Railway a 4–4–0 locomotive of class L12 (No. 412) took over a special train at Templecombe for a non-stop run to Waterloo. The train ran down from Dinton to Wilton at a speed of 70 miles an hour. At Salisbury West, Driver W. J. Robins hung on the whistle and came streaking through the station. At this point he should have reduced speed to not more than 30 miles an hour to take a curve of 10 chains radius but instead he carried on unslacked, with the result that his train left the rails and ploughed through a goods train.

Robins is said to have been a teetotaller, so inebriation is ruled out. Whatever the reason, it led to his death and that of his fireman and more than twenty others. The inspecting officer recommended that the 30 miles an hour restriction should be reduced to 15 m.p.h. and in recent years it has been further reduced to 10 m.p.h.

Be British

THE South Eastern and Chatham Railway had, just prior to the 1914-18 war, ordered ten new locomotives from a German firm and these were delivered in May 1914 with a proviso that payment was due three months after delivery subject to satisfactory performance. The payment became due on the very day that war was declared and it was not possible to make it until six years later. With typical British fair play the company added interest to the amount due.

Who Threw That Chalk?

IN December 1915 a fall of chalk from the famous white cliffs of Dover completely blocked the railway line of the South Eastern and Chatham Railway. This was during the first world war and so extensive was the blockage, that the line remained closed until after the end of the war.

Tunnel Full Of Ammo

ON THE London, Brighton and South Coast Railway on the 18th April 1918 a goods train from Eastbourne divided in Redhill Tunnel, leaving three wagons and the brake in the tunnel. The occurrence was not noticed by the signalling staff with the result that a further goods train was allowed to enter the section. This ran into the vehicles standing in the tunnel, derailing them and its own engine and leading wagons. Then came a down goods carrying ammunition (it was wartime) which ran into the derailed stock and filled the tunnel to the roof with wreckage.

The tunnel was clear for traffic in less than two days.

Personal Service

SIR JOHN Tyrell, a landowner near Chelmsford, asked as added compensation for selling land to the Eastern Counties Railway, the right to have a private station and the right to stop any train he chose. When this was granted in 1843 no very great inconvenience was caused to the relatively light traffic but as the gentleman lived for a further 34 years it became quite an embarrassment to the railway company.

When Sir John died the company exercised remarkable restraint by doing nothing until after the funeral—then they moved in and the station disappeared without trace.

A Railway With The Bailiffs In

IN 1867 the Great Eastern Railway company was in financial difficulties and some of its locomotives bore notices to indicate that they were the property of creditors.

Twopence Return

WHEN THE Great Eastern Railway company moved its London terminus from Bishopsgate to Liverpool Street it was necessary to demolish a large number of working-class dwellings, the occupants being re-housed in outlying districts. To recompense these people for the additional distance they had to travel to their employment, the company was obliged by Act of

Parliament to provide trains at a fare of twopence return. Some people thus rode upwards of twenty miles each day for two pence—quite cheap even for those days.

Nothing But Trouble

ON THE 6th August 1883 a train bound for Gravesend had just got beyond Dartford when it ran over a donkey which had strayed on to the line. It took a considerable time to extricate the body of the dead animal from beneath the locomotive, but eventually this was accomplished and the train proceeded.

It had just got moving when a passing balloon ran into difficulties and dropped on to the line so closely in front of the advancing train that death seemed certain for the two men in the balloon basket. However, by some miracle the balloon gained some buoyancy in the nick of time and lifted into a nearby field.

Overhead Propulsion

IN 1915 a Zeppelin chased after a Great Eastern Railway train near Bury St. Edmunds and aimed five bombs upon it—none hit the train.

Things That Go Bump In The Dark

CANONBURY Tunnel was on a London suburban branch line connecting the Great Northern Railway and the North London Railway. It had at its north end a signal box (Finsbury Park No. 1) belonging to the G. N. Railway and at its south end a box (Canonbury Junction) belonging to the N. L. Railway.

On the morning of the 10th December 1881, when the rush hour trains were coming along every few minutes, the signal-man at Canonbury Junction found it necessary to hold a train and, on being offered another train by the Finsbury Park man, he rang back six bells for "line not clear" followed by seven bells. The man at Finsbury Park did not recognise this signal as it did not come in G.N. practice at all, but he had a North

London code book handy and found that seven bells was "permissive block". Not wanting to cause any delay for which he might later be censured, he sent his second train through the tunnel under caution, and it bumped into the back of the first train although no damage was done. When a third train came along, Finsbury Park No. 1 offered it and Canonbury Junction sent back six bells followed by seven bells. So Finsbury sent this one into the tunnel under caution as well—and it bumped into the second train, again with little or no damage.

The passengers, meantime, had decided that all these bumps in the darkness were unnatural and they all started to climb down on to the track just as a fourth train entered the tunnel— under caution, of course. But the driver of this train was not perhaps quite so cautious as he might have been because his impact with train number three caused him to leave the metals. One of the guards eventually got out into the daylight at the north end of the tunnel just in time to wave down train number five and to stop the Finsbury Park signalman from his misdoings.

Shortly after this the Railway Clearing House Committee considered the advisability of standardising signal codes and some uniformity was introduced.

The Compleat History

SIMPLY because every other book on railway history which I have ever read (or nearly) has contained this story I feel that I would be tempting fate were I not to include it here!

Edmund Denison, chairman of the Great Northern Railway, once said that the company's line ended in a ploughed field four miles north of Doncaster.

Roast Beef Of Old England

IN Welwyn North Tunnel on the Great Northern Railway on the 9th June 1866 a down GNR goods train had an engine failure in the tunnel. This piece of line gave running rights also to the Midland Railway and on this occasion a down MR goods ran into the failed train and the wreckage blocked both roads. Soon after this an up GNR train well-laden with meat for the London markets ploughed into the debris. The wreckage caught fire from the scattered coals of the locomotives and it is said that the smell of good roast beef filled the neighbourhood for several days.

Don't Neglect The Paper Work

AT Bawtry on the Great Northern Railway one day in 1879 the *Flying Scotsman,* hauled by Stirling locomotive No. 215 (a single driver), suffered a broken axle on the second coach while bowling through the station at 60 miles an hour. Two coaches were derailed. The coach in which the fault occurred had been in use for eleven years but no one knew how many miles it had run and it had not been regularly examined. It appears that the flaw was one which could and ought to have been detected long before the accident. There were no deaths and little injury.

Sinners All?

THE Grand Junction Railway Act, 1833, stipulates that no clergyman may be a director of the company.

Railway Sports

NAVVIES engaged on railway construction necessarily lived on the job and found many novel ways of entertaining themselves during their off-duty hours. During the building of the Kilsby Tunnel on the London and North Western Railway they fell into the habit of leaping across the top of the working shafts. The penalty for failure was a rapid descent of up to 160 feet and two or three fell to their deaths.

Why Crewe?

CREWE Works was built by the Grand Junction Railway Company in the wilds of the Cheshire countryside where no town existed. The company had perforce to build a town to house and provide for the thousands of men who would work there. It was called Crewe in honour of the Marquis of Crewe who lived at Crewe Hall nearby.

The Great Provider

THE railway authorities at Crewe made provision for the supply of gas and water to what was originally a one hundred per cent railway town. Times changed and the town expanded, but the railway continued to supply water until just before the last war. Gas was still being supplied when that industry was nationalised in 1952.

Strange Freight

THERE IS a report in 1887 of a tiger being lost on the railway somewhere between Wolverton and Rugby: "When found, forward to Liverpool."

Dis-Connected Rod

A TRAIN of the London & North Western Railway was passing Weedon on the 14th August 1915 when the offside connecting rod came adrift and severely damaged the adjoining down road. The Irish Mail was approaching at great speed and became derailed before any action could be taken to stop it. Ten persons were killed.

Snakes Alive – And Dead

IN 1958 a boy who was travelling between Birmingham and Stourbridge allowed his pet snake to escape, whereupon it rapidly slid into the upholstery of the seat. A search by railway staff failed to locate the reptile and the compartment was locked before the train completed its journey. The carriage was sent to Cardiff and the upholstery was taken out but there was still no sign of the snake. Eventually the carriage passed through the disinfestation chamber at Swindon. This made the snake come out of his hiding hole but he was dead when found.

Glenfield Tunnel

THIS TUNNEL on the Leicester and Swannington Railway was a trifle troublesome in its early days. On the 5th April

1831 a contractor named Daniel Jowett fell down one of the shafts and was killed. On the 17th July in the following year the first train was sent through the tunnel hauled by the locomotive *Comet*. The tunnel arch was insufficiently high (or the locomotive chimney was insufficiently low) and these two pieces of railway equipment came into violent contact!

Do You Want To Believe It?

AT A level crossing near Thornton on the Leicester and Swannington Railway there occurred, on the 4th May 1833, a relatively trivial accident wherein a locomotive collided with a horse and cart. What is strange is that this accident has been argued about and written about probably more than any other in railway history.

It is claimed by some that, as a sequel to this event, the steam trumpet (steam whistle) was invented as a warning of approach. It is also said that this was perfected by a musical instrument maker and the prototype sent to Newcastle where new locomotives were being made.

There are others who say that this story is complete rubbish. You can believe it if you wish.

Just The Ticket

THE Leicester and Swannington Railway was the first to speed up the issuing of passenger tickets by abandoning the complicated booking of passengers' names, time of journey, preference for inside or outside, etc., which was a relic of the stage coach age.

On this railway in 1832 a system of brass tokens was introduced whereby the passenger received a token in exchange for the fare and handed it in at the end of the journey. It was then returned to the issuing station for use again. A number of other railways introduced similar systems but about ten years later the Edmondson pasteboard tickets were beginning to come into general use.

Landslip At Bugsworth

THE AUTUMN of 1866 was extremely wet throughout the country and many railways suffered, as did much of the countryside, by the ground becoming completely sodden and almost fluid. At Bugsworth in Derbyshire on the Midland Railway, a bridge, a viaduct and an embankment disintegrated. The station building was damaged and some nearby farmsteads completely collapsed. Sixteen acres of land slid down the hill to the river which was thus diverted in its course. The Midland Railway company employed 400 men for ten weeks in repairing the damage and traffic resumed in February 1867.

The Midland also had to rebuild their Apperley viaduct in Yorkshire which was affected by the same floods.

Cheap At The Price

AT A meeting of Midland Railway employees held in Leicester on the 23rd November 1886, a signalman stated that he had just come off a thirteen hour night shift during which he had passed 148 trains, made 500 lever movements, 1600 bell beats and 2,300 dial signals. His pay for this work was 3s. 9½d.

Peace Out Of The Window

CHARLES Peace, the notorious murderer, was being conveyed on January 22nd, 1879, by the Great Northern Railway to Sheffield where he was to stand trial, when he contrived to make his escape by diving through the carriage window while the train was hurtling through the Nottinghamshire countryside. One of his attendants managed to catch him by one leg and thus held him head downwards for several miles. Eventually Peace struggled free and fell to the ground. He was found to be injured, but ultimately stood trial and was hanged.

Northern England

Good Morning, Brother Mole

DURING THE building of the Liverpool and Manchester Railway, George Stephenson chanced to be inspecting the Edge Hill Tunnel at Liverpool when he was amazed to see a face peering at him from a hole in the tunnel roof. This turned out to be a wealthy eccentric whose property stood above the tunnel and who had been so fascinated by this method of passing through the bowels of the earth that he had indulged in considerable tunnelling activity on his own account. One gathers that he was highly delighted to have met with the professionals in such intimate proximity.

Stephenson's Rocket

THE *Rocket* won the prize of £500 offered by the directors of the Liverpool and Manchester Railway in the Rainhill competition in 1829. It was a four-wheeled engine and with a full boiler it weighed $4\frac{1}{4}$ tons; with the loaded tender it was $7\frac{1}{2}$ tons. The boiler was 6 feet long and 3 feet 4 inches in diameter. It had 25 three-inch copper boiler tubes through which the flames passed to the 12-inch chimney. The heating surface was $117\frac{3}{4}$ square feet and there were two cylinders of 8 inches diameter and $16\frac{1}{2}$ inches stroke. The driving wheels were 4 feet $8\frac{1}{2}$ inches. Exhaust steam passed into the chimney to improve the draught. On its trial the *Rocket* reached 24 miles an hour.

The conditions laid down for the competition were:
1. The engine must consume its own smoke.
2. If the engine weigh 6 tons, it must draw after it 20 tons at 10 miles an hour; the pressure on the gauge not to exceed 50 lbs.

3. There must be two safety valves, the engine and boiler must be supported on springs and rest on six wheels, the height of the whole not to exceed 15 feet to the top of the chimney.
4. It must not weigh more than 6 tons, less weight preferred, which may draw a less weight behind it, then it may have four wheels.
5. The price not to exceed £550.

Not Parotitis

AMONG the curiously named stations on Britain's railways, surely the most curious is Oldham Mumps. This is not named after some childish illness but after the district of Mumps, which from the eighteenth century was a village near Oldham and derived its name from the beggars or "mumpers" who frequented the vicinity. There was an ancient bridge and a brook bearing the same name.

Tar For A Railroad

WHEN the Midland Railway was being built between Leeds and Bradford it passed by the Bradford gasworks. At that time the only by-product from the production of gas which could be put to use was the coke, and many thousands of pounds worth of good tar were dumped on the site of the new railway to get the required levels.

Persona Non Grata

DURING the building of the Keighley and Worth Valley Railway in 1865 the engineers were making a tunnel at Ingrow when they penetrated a stratum of quicksand. The removal of this, and the pile-driving which then became necessary to support the tunnel, disturbed the ground above and led to serious damage to a newly built Wesleyan Chapel.

The chapel had to be demolished and rebuilt, and after going to arbitration the railway company had to pay damages of £1,980. The foundation stone of the original chapel had been laid by Sir Isaac Holden, a leading Wesleyan of the district, but possibly because he also happened to be chairman of the railway company he was not selected to perform a similar function for the replacement building.

Winkers

THE Furness Railway instituted a system whereby its distant signals showed a *flashing* red light after dark.

Interment Of A Locomotive

PART OF the line of the Furness Railway between Lindal and Ulverston which was on a high embankment subsided on the 22nd September 1892 at a point over an old mine. At first the hole was thirty feet deep and the first sign of its appearance was during the morning when Driver Postlethwaite took his goods train over the line. He noticed cracks appearing in the ground, shut off steam, jumped off the engine and injured himself in so doing. As he got clear the ground opened up and the engine was swallowed, leaving the tender above ground.

Attempts were made to widen the cavity in the hope of hauling the engine out but by three o'clock in the afternoon the ground began to move again and the engine sank to about sixty feet below rail level. Passengers had to walk between shuttle services running to either side of the subsidence and goods traffic had to make a detour of about 100 miles. It could not be ascertained how deep the engine eventually settled and it was written off as lost. Heavy rains may have contributed to the incident.

Underground Fire On The Overhead!

DINGLE station was situated in the "dead end" of a tunnel at the southern extremity of the Liverpool Overhead Railway. On 23rd December 1901 an evening rush hour train approached the station with one of the electric traction motors overheating. This eventually caused the train to come to a stand some yards short of the platform so the driver several times attempted to restart, each attempt being accompanied by severe arcing at the defective motor. This eventually set the train on fire. Most of the passengers got clear along the track, through the station and up the subway to the open air. Six persons who had apparently tarried to fight the fire lost their lives.

The draught through the tunnel kept the fire burning furiously and, being associated with electrical equipment, there was a good deal of acrid smoke. The confined space undoubtedly maintained a very high temperature in the fire, thus rendering the plight of those trapped a hopeless one.

Going Down

ON THE 28th April 1953 the roof of Clifton Hall Tunnel, near Manchester, collapsed at a point where there had been a shaft which was later filled in. The houses which had been built over the in-fill fell down the hole causing five deaths.

Oldest

THE OLDEST railway bridge in the world is said to be the Causey Arch, near Stanley in County Durham. It is 60 feet high, has a span of over 100 feet and is over 200 years old. It was built in 1727 by Ralph Wood as part of the old Tanfield wagonway which was later incorporated into the Brandling Junction Railway.

Engine Afloat

THE well-known locomotive of the very early years of steam railways, *Wylam Dilly*, was rigged up on a boat and fitted with paddles to act as a tug on the river Tyne during a strike of watermen in 1822.

These New-Fangled Engines

THE Newcastle and Carlisle Railway Act of 1829 prohibited the use of locomotives but by the time the line opened in 1835 these machines had been improved to such a standard that it would have been folly not to use them. The directors therefore decided to open the line on the 9th March using steam engines.

Unfortunately a local person lodged an objection and services had to be suspended, but public opinion was sympathetic to the railway and the objector was persuaded to stand down. The line then resumed its service and Parliament eventually granted the necessary amendment to make the use of locomotives legal.

Parliament Perplexed

BY Section 114 of the Whitby and Pickering Railway Act, 1833, the company was authorised to use locomotives, but Section 134 of the Act forbade their use!

Brakes Aflame

THE Ingleby incline on the North Yorkshire and Cleveland Railway was on a gradient of 1 in 5 and, as the traffic consisted of wagons of ironstone descending from the mines, the incline was worked by gravity under the control of a brake in the drum-house at the top. One day in June 1869 the brake over-heated by friction and the whole building went up in flames.

Wreckers

IN THE 1880s there was, of course, no electric floodlighting and the contractors on the Whitby, Redcar and Middlesbrough Union Railway used bonfires to provide illumination for the night shift. On one occasion during construction on the cliffs overlooking the North Sea, the captain of a ship mistook the fires for the lights of Whitby and ran aground at the foot of the cliffs.

Ignorance Is Bliss

A double-headed express passenger train crashed into the rear of a freight train near Northallerton on the 4th October 1894. The accident was caused by the driver of the train engine believing that the driver of the pilot was in charge, whereas the pilot considered that as he was merely providing extra power he had no responsibility for the running of the train. The result was that they both ran on in blissful ignorance of the adverse signals they were passing.

Interment Of A Viaduct

A LINE of the North Eastern Railway which crossed Kilton viaduct had to be taken out of use in 1911 when local iron-stone mining affected the foundations of the arches rendering them unsafe. The remedy was found in converting the viaduct into an embankment by tipping about three-quarters of a million tons of spoil from the heaps around the mines. The viaduct was not removed but remains embedded in the embankment. The line came back into full use in 1913.

Tunnel in a Churchyard

THIS monument, which stands in Otley churchyard in York-shire, was erected at the expense of the contractor and others engaged on the building of the Leeds and Thirsk Railway, as a memorial to those who were killed during the construction of the Bramhope Tunnel. It is in the form of a model of the tunnel.

Egg Strike

ON July 4th, 1913, at Leeds station, a hen, which was in transit with others of the same feather, laid an egg in its crate. A porter who noticed this removed the egg lest it should get broken, whereupon a railway policeman arrested him. His mates were out on strike within minutes, but when their superior ordered the man's release all just as quickly returned to normal.

An Odd Railway

THE Spurn Head Railway was provided by the War Department as a means of communication between Kilnsea (Yorkshire) and the Spurn Point lighthouse and coastguard station, a distance of three miles. It was opened about 1919 and closed in 1951. Although at one time the line had five locomotives, it boasted some very odd vehicles, one being a flat trolley with a mast and sail. A fair turn of speed could be achieved with a following wind, and the Revd. Alfred Poulsom states that on one occasion he had a hair-raising ride as the only brake in evidence was a chunk of wood which was dropped off in front of the wheels.

Who's Cheating?

IT IS said that when two tank engines, Nos 855 and 856 of the London and North Eastern Railway, were taken into Darlington Works in 1939, the former was intended to be scrapped and the latter overhauled for further service. But they broke up the wrong engine!

Whether or not this mistake ever became known to those in authority is not disclosed, but the records were kept straight by overhauling No. 855 and renumbering it as No. 856. This later became B.R. No. 69376.

Unexploded Bomb

A TRAIN running from Hull to Scarborough on the 11th November 1941 was hit by a German bomb which did not explode but penetrated the tender and leading carriage before falling on the track. The train passed over it safely but later came to a stand through lack of water, the tender tank having been pierced.

Wales

A Victorian "Hot Line"

ON THE 7th January 1862 a messenger carrying Government dispatches from the area of the American Civil War stepped ashore at Holyhead at 8.15 a.m. and was whisked away by the London and North Western Railway to arrive at Euston at 1.13 p.m.—an average speed of about 53 miles an hour. This was a masterpiece of organisation as it was not known to within many hours what time the ship would arrive. Engines were changed with but the loss of an odd minute and a cab was waiting at Euston to take the messenger to Whitehall.

Who's In Charge?

IN 1865, when railway discipline was strict, Stationmaster J. Baddiley of the Cambrian Railways left his station without nominating someone to take charge. For this oversight he lost his job.

A Dramatic Conflagration

ON THE London and North Western Railway at Abergele on a day in 1868, some shunting work was being carried out at the top of a 1 in 100 gradient. A brake van was placed on the main line with the brake applied and four wagons of paraffin oil were buffed up to it, but it failed to hold to the brake and all five vehicles sped down the hill meeting the Irish Mail train at some considerable speed. The paraffin was sprayed liberally over the engine and the leading four coaches.

It ignited instantly and caused a most serious fire in which 32 passengers lost their lives.

It's No Use Saying "Sorry"

THE DRIVER of a freight train on the Cambrian Railway on the 25th November 1869 was unable to stop at adverse signals at Carno. He ran through the station colliding with the special train of the company chairman, Lord Vane.

One does not knock the company chairman with impunity so both the driver and the stationmaster were sacked.

Knowing The Ropes

PERHAPS I may be permitted to include here a personal reminiscence. It is historical, I suppose, because it concerns my grandmother and goes back to the years just after the first world war.

I had an aunt who lived near Rhosllanerchrugog in North Wales and from time to time my grandmother would pay a visit, leaving Chester at about 7.15 a.m. (workmen's ticket, of course) and in due course arriving at Wrexham. From there the journey continued in a "motor train" which was the usual name for the G.W.R. push-and-pull trains on the local branch lines.

On one occasion my grandmother took me on this journey and, being a cold morning, she looked in the waiting room at Wrexham to see if there was a fire. There was not, so we took our seats in the motor train which was in the platform. When the man eventually came to examine our tickets we were well on the way to Moss, which was on another branch altogether. We were told we should have to stay on the train until it returned to Wrexham, but this did not dismay my grandmother who knew that the self-same set would then proceed to Rhosllanerchrugog and we should have waited in the warm train rather than the chill waiting room.

"I usually do that on a cold morning", she said, "but you have to pretend to be surprised that you are on the wrong train".

Scotland

Special To Oblivion

ONE EVENING in March 1845 a passenger missed his train from Glasgow for Edinburgh and chartered a special to take him on his journey. This consisted of a small, leaky engine and one carriage. No guard was provided and the driver forgot to hang on a tail lamp. The engine could not even maintain sufficient steam to drag itself and its carriage along the road to Edinburgh and made frequent stops. The result was that it was overtaken and run into by a following train which shattered the carriage and killed the passenger.

The driver and the locomotive superintendent were brought to justice. The driver was sentenced to nine months for neglecting his duty by not using a tail lamp and the locomotive superintendent was awarded twelve months for culpable homicide.

"The Train Now Standing In The Hut . . . . "

WHEN THE Caledonian Railway was under construction it was decided that their headquarters city of Edinburgh should be graced with a magnificent station. Accordingly, a station was planned and the foundation stone laid on the 9th April 1847. As railway capital was exceedingly hard to raise at this time no further stones were laid and the Caledonian had to manage with a wooden hut, albeit a fair sized one 180 feet long. This was their principal station for the next 22 years.

An Execution On A Railway

ON THE 14th May 1841 the, as yet unfinished, Edinburgh & Glasgow Railway witnessed a macabre scene when two railway labourers were hanged in view of their workmates for murdering the foreman. The foreman had sacked an Irish labourer some months previously and he, to seek his revenge, had enlisted the aid of his brother and another labourer who were both employed in the construction of the railway. Next day these two went to work with iron bars in their possession and, as the foreman leaned over the parapet of a bridge in the super-intendence of some work, they set about him with fatal results. They were tried and found guilty and it was felt that a public execution at the scene of their crime would have a salutory effect upon the labouring fraternity and teach them that such violence would not be tolerated.

Dead Drunk

ON THE Granton branch line on the 8th July 1860 a driver and four of his cronies got very drunk and went for a spin on an engine. This ended up in the sea, drowning four of the wayward party.

Pressure Point

ON THE railway network of the Dalmellington Iron Company there occurred an accident in 1868 which illustrates that even a steam locomotive can only be abused for so long before it retaliates.

It had been the practice for drivers to hold down the safety valves in order to get extra pressure in readiness for moving heavy trains up gradients. When Driver Gill did this with his little 0-4-0 tank engine the rivets of the dome gave way. The dome and safety valves of this engine were on top of the firebox and they and the driver were thrown into the middle of the next field. It is reported that in spite of this experience, in which he was badly scalded, Gill continued to get a bit of extra pressure by holding down the safety valves, as indeed did many other drivers of the period.

Cheers!

QUEEN Victoria, travelling in Scotland on the 6th September 1872, was greeted at Bonar Bridge by the Duke of Sutherland, this being the boundary of his territory. It was also the commencement of the Sutherland Railway, but the Queen noted in her diary that the Duke had been driving the engine (!) all the way from Inverness and had only here presented himself to her.

While this was going on the Bonar Bridge stationmaster would not leave the crowd in peace but kept telling them to cheer and cheer again without ceasing.

A Chance Missed

THE PROMOTERS of the Dingwall and Skye Railway met considerable opposition from landowners around Strathpeffer when laying out their line, with the result that this railway passed a couple of miles from the town instead of going through it as intended. This also took the line through more difficult country and necessitated more severe gradients. At a later date the inhabitants regretted this state of affairs and a branch line had to be built to give rail communication for this popular spa.

How A Railway Lost A Ship

THE Highland Railway Company (and the Dingwall and Skye Railway before it) owned two steamships for its service from Strome Ferry to Portree on the Isle of Skye together with the odd trip to points such as Stornaway. Eventually it was found that the traffic then coming forward only justified the use of one ship. The good ship *Ferret* was therefore withdrawn from service and advertised as being available for charter.

In October 1880 a firm of brokers made an approach to the company regarding the charter of the ship on behalf of a Mr. Smith who was said to be related to the First Lord of the Admiralty and who wished to take his wife to the Mediterranean for the good of her health. The company took up the references which had been quoted and as these were satisfactory the ship was handed over in exchange for three months charter fee paid in advance. The *Ferret* stocked up at Glasgow and sailed south, taking on coal at Cardiff on her way to the Mediterranean.

At the end of three months the company applied to the brokers for a further payment of charter fee as the ship had not returned. It was then found that the firm of brokers (Henderson and Co.) did not exist and the ship itself appeared to have completely vanished from the face of the earth (or the face of the sea!). It was some months later that news came of a ship answering the description of the *Ferret* (but named *India*) being offered for sale at Melbourne, Australia. Certain suspicious circumstances caused enquires to be made which established that no such ship as the *India* was registered and that it was indeed the *Ferret* in disguise.

It seems that the captain, the purser and the man called Smith had picked up valuable cargoes in Brazil by means of forged documents and then transported them to South Africa where the goods were sold profitably. The next step was to sell the ship as well and clear out with a very handsome bank balance. However, the port authorities at Melbourne seized the ship on 17th April 1881 and the miscreants were brought to justice. The agent of the Highland Railway then sold the ship quite legitimately to the Adelaide Steamship Company who ran her for another forty years.

But Not On Sundays

MANY PEOPLE in Victorian days held the view that Sunday should be kept as a day of rest and this feeling was particularly strong in Scotland.

On Sunday the 3rd June 1883 it was proposed to run a special fish train from Strome Ferry, on a line normally closed on Sundays. The local people, on hearing of this, took matters into their own hands and, armed with various offensive weapons, prevented the fish from being landed. They took possession of the quay and the station and effectively repelled the efforts of the police and railway officials to dislodge them. The assembled multitude then sang hymns and prayed for the souls of the railway directors until midnight. It then being Monday, they surrendered possession of the premises and normal working was resumed. Some of the leaders of this disturbance were arrested and committed to prison in Edinburgh.

Greasy Rails

ON THE 21st July 1887 at Bishopbriggs on the North British Railway, a passenger train which was checked by signals had stood for some time when a second passenger train collided with the rear. On investigation it was found that the brakes had been applied but had had no apparent effect in bringing the train to a halt. While this mystery was being discussed a third train bowled merrily into the rear of the other two. The reason for this collision was the same as before.

Eventually it was found that the original signal check was for a freight train which had been stopped somewhere ahead for examination because a barrel of oil was leaking. The oil, thus liberally sprayed on the track for miles back, had played havoc with the braking propensities of following trains.

Elementary Physics

DURING THE building of the Forth Bridge a visitor was allowed to descend into one of the pneumatic caissons in which men were working on the underwater foundations. In such a caisson the air is compressed to withstand the pressures of the water without. The visitor was very impressed with all that he saw and, taking out his hip flask, offered drinks to all around. When the flask was empty he corked it and returned it to his pocket. On returning to the surface he overlooked the fact that the flask was now filled with compressed air and it exploded with a considerable bang.

Vital Statistics!

THE Forth Bridge scheme cost £3,000,000 altogether, of which £1,700,000 was for the bridge itself. The length of the metal part of the bridge is one mile. It includes 54,000 tons of steel, of which 4,000 tons is accounted for by the 6,500,000 rivets. 21,000 tons of cement were used and the masonry and concrete totals 138,000 cubic yards. To paint the bridge requires more than 50 tons of paint and the total area to be painted is 135 acres. The total allowance for expansion and contraction is 8ft. 4ins.

Coming Down The Mountain

ACHNASHELLACH on the Dingwall and Skye Railway saw an accident on the 14th October 1892 of a kind which appears to be not uncommon. A mixed train halted on a gradient for shunting purposes and, when the engine was detached, the brakes failed to hold the train with the result that it ran away down the bank and up the other side of the valley.

It was late afternoon and had become dark but the engine driver, perceiving what had happened, set off after his train. As he got to the bottom of the hill going in one direction, he met his train coming down again in the other direction. The impact was considerable and eight passengers were seriously injured.

Knowing The Ropes

THE Glasgow District Subway Railway, $6\frac{1}{2}$ miles long, was designed to be operated by cable traction. It was the only underground railway in the world to employ this type of motive power and it operated successfully for 38 years until electrification in 1935.

Unfair To Loco Superintendents

F. G. Smith, Locomotive Superintendent of the Highland Railway from 1911 to 1915, lost his job in singular circumstances. He is said to have been a very capable engineer and, to meet pressing traffic needs, he designed and had built a new class of 4-6-0 locomotive weighing over 72 tons. When the civil engineer got to hear about this he declared that some of his bridges would not bear the weight and consequently the engines could not be used. The directors were more than a little annoyed about this and asked Mr. Smith to resign—which he did.

Incidentally, the Highland sold the engines to the Caledonian at a profit. After the Grouping, they found their way back on to the Highland—and the bridges did not collapse.

Making Tracks Quickly

DURING THE 1914-1918 war the Highland Railway was called upon to carry a fantastic amount of additional traffic for various Admiralty establishments, and in 1915 it became necessary to lay an additional branch from Inverness to the harbour. It was requested that this should be ready within six weeks. However, the requirement seems to have been taken not too seriously and work had not started when the message came through that the Admiralty had sent off the first train from the South of England for this branch. With remarkable speed the line was ready by the time the train arrived!

The Worst Accident

THE Quintinshill accident is frequently mentioned in railway literature but it is not often that the details are given—it is presumably taken for granted that the well-read enthusiast will know all about it anyway.

This accident occurred at Quintinshill near Gretna on the 22nd May 1915. It was wartime and the railways were carrying a lot of extra traffic, some of it being of a priority nature. On this morning the signalman at Quintinshill had his siding full with waiting freights and, in order to get a local train out of the way for some down expresses, he had to cross it over to the up line to wait.

The signalmen were changing shifts at the time and men from the various waiting trains had reported to the box, so that, for one reason or another, there were eleven men in the signalbox. It is always difficult to say why any accident happens, but somehow a troop train was accepted in the up direction even though the local was standing on that line right outside the window.

The troop train contained half a battalion of the Royal Scots, consisting of 498 officers and men, on their way to Liverpool to join a ship which would take them out to the fighting in the Dardanelles. The troop special ploughed into the local and within one minute an express on the down line ran at speed into the wreckage and escaping passengers. The accident also affected the waiting trains on adjacent lines.

This accident is outstanding for the number of lives lost, 227, the number of trains involved (five) and the fact that the gas lighting equipment contributed to the fire which raged into the next day. Incidentally, the other half of the battalion which travelled in another train suffered much loss of life in the fighting.

How Odd

INVERNESS station, although on the main line to the north of Scotland, has no platforms on that line but stands at right angles to it, trains having to curve in from either direction. Through trains are worked in a way which is disconcerting to the uninformed traveller. The train appears to ignore the station and goes some distance past it before stopping and propelling back into the appropriate platform.

Beating The Mail

THE DIRECT route from the Lowlands of Scotland north to Inverness originally ran over the metals of several railways and at Aberdeen this necessitated a walk, or a cab, from Guild Street station to the Waterloo station of the Great North of Scotland Railway about half a mile away.

Now if the train from the south arrived late, which it often did, the G.N. of S. was obliged to wait for the mails but was not so assiduous in considering the convenience of passengers. Thus the streets would echo to the hurried footsteps of passengers desperately trying to arrive at Waterloo as quickly as the mail van, for as soon as the mail was aboard the train would depart and the barriers would be closed in the very faces of the advancing passengers from the south.

Ireland

Heads You Lose

ON THE 26th February 1842 a passenger in an open third class carriage of the Ulster Railway decided to climb up and seat himself on the roof of the next carriage. At that time the guards travelled on a roof-top seat and this passenger was seen by the guard who walked along the roofs to remonstrate with him. While standing there to see the passenger safely down, the guard was struck on the head by an overbridge and was found to be dead on arrival at the next station.

Weightlessness

IN 1843 the line from Kingstown to Dalkey in Ireland opened with the atmospheric system of traction. One day a student engineer named Ebrington made a test run on the line but omitted to couple the train to the piston carriage. The lack of weight caused the piston carriage and the young man to be whisked away at something over 80 miles an hour and to fly into Dalkey Station "like a cork out of a pop-gun".

An Elopement On The Wrong Lines

THE Portadown and Dungannon Railway provided an unusual derailment on the 9th September 1858. The train was wrongly diverted into a siding and, pushing through the stopping blocks, dived into a peat bog. But the reason for the diversion is interesting!

A young lady of Annaghmore was in love with a railway engine driver but her father disapproved of the match. Determined to elope they arranged that the young lady should be at the station on this day to be whisked away by her lover on his fiery steed. Her father had somehow become acquainted with the scheme and he designed to stop it. The staff of Annaghmore station were about equally divided in taking sides in the affair, so that while one man was helping the girl up on to the train at the side away from the platform another had gone forward to throw over the points so that the train should run into a siding and be unable to escape before the irate father should arrive.

Unfortunately, the driver, on seeing his betrothed safely aboard, gave the engine full regulator to get away quickly but failed to notice where he was heading. The train landed in the bog and the thwarted couple were considerably dampened in more ways than one.

Buried Treasure

IT IS believed that a crate of champagne lies beneath the one-time railway yard at Ballycastle. When the line was opened the yard was incomplete and a crate of the ceremonial drink was misappropriated and hidden beneath the rubble to be carried home later. Unfortunately, and before he could recover his loot, the miscreant was moved to another station and the champagne became well and truly covered as the construction of the yard was completed. It is still there if anyone cares to dig for it!

Time Will Tell

AN ACCIDENT occurred on the Londonderry and Lough Swilly Railway near Fahan on the 17th September 1889 when a train became derailed because a p.w. gang had removed a rail for renewal. The gang had neither watch nor timetable and it was later discovered that the man in charge was unable to tell the time anyway.

Irish Ingenuity

IT IS SAID that the Listowel and Ballybunnion railway once had to transport a piano, and because all loads had to be balanced on this unique monorail railway a cow was loaded into the other side as ballast. The problem then was to get the cow back to the starting point and this was done by balancing it with two calves which were later loaded into opposite sides to get them back where they belonged!

Cold Sober, Begorrah!

THE County Donegal Railways are credited with many amusing stories and among these is the one about the Sunday train on the 7th September 1913. Yes, only one train, for the Sunday service in those days consisted of a train from Strabane to Londonderry during the morning and the return of the same train in the evening. This entailed leaving it for some hours at Londonderry, during which period the members of the crew were free to do as they pleased.

On this day they claimed to have spent a lazy day reading, but there were those who said that they had obviously been enjoying quite convivial company. However that may be, they decided on the return journey to see what the engine was capable of and, in turning into a passing loop at Donemana at 40 m.p.h., they toppled part of the train over on to its side with the loss of one life. The driver earned four months hard labour for his misdeed.

Red Tape

THE Great Northern Railway of Ireland had lines in both the north and south, which meant that after the inauguration of the Irish Free State (Eire) this railway ran in two different countries. Eventually both countries nationalised their railways and they set up a Joint Board to operate the GNR(I).

In 1955 and 1956 a number of unremunerative lines were closed and the Northern Minister of Commerce advertised even more closures which would have had repercussions throughout the system. These drastic proposals were referred to the Transport Tribunals in both Northern Ireland and Eire. Strangely the Northern government, which had in fact proposed the closures, did not attend the enquiry or send any evidence to support its case. Such evidence as was put forward by other organisations was overwhelmingly against closure. It was said that the introduction of diesel traction, which had long been delayed, would turn the alleged losses into a working surplus.

The Northern Transport Tribunal rejected the evidence and recommended closure, while in the south the Tribunal gave a fair review of the evidence and advised against closure. So in 1957 about a quarter of the GNR(I) system was closed contrary to the advice of the management and others regarded as competent to judge the issue. Thus the closure of some of the northern lines and connections had effects in the south and in turn forced closures there.

Railway Quartermasters

DURING the Crimean War the British Army found itself in some difficulty in organising the provisioning and supply of the troops, partly because of the distance from this country and partly because of the difficult terrain between the coast and the troops.

Rescue came in the shape of that well-known firm of railway contractors, Peto, Brassey and Betts, who had become accustomed to sending out equipment and supplies to large construction gangs in many parts of the world and in organising their "armies" of navvies. They put a couple of dozen steamships to work, got thousands of tons of equipment and supplies on the move and built many miles of railway, all within a few weeks.

Railwaymen Prisoners Of War

ON THE 4th August 1914 three steam ships of the Great Central Railway were at Hamburg on the company's service from Grimsby. It was becoming obvious that the war was about to start—in fact war was declared at mid-night — and the masters of the vessels decided to return to this country with all speed. They were intercepted by a German gun-boat and returned to Hamburg where the crews were interned and the ships pressed into German war service.

A Right Royal Engine Driver

IN October 1934, King Boris of Bulgaria was travelling in a train in that country when an accident occurred on the footplate, resulting in the driver becoming injured and his clothing catching fire. The king was made of sterner stuff than the officials on the train and rushed to the rescue. It was believed that the king's action saved the man's life.

The problem then was to get the train on to the end of its journey, and again His Majesty came to the rescue because he happened to be an experienced driver. He took over the controls for the remainder of the journey.

Quite A Journey

THE Trans-Siberian Express from Leningrad to Vladivostock takes nine days to travel the 5,971 miles between these towns.

Casey Jones

BORN IN 1864 at Cayce, Kentucky (hence his nickname), John Luther Jones started his working life as an apprentice telegrapher on the Mobile and Ohio Railroad. On the 1st March 1888 he moved on to the Illinois Central Railroad as a fireman and in 1890 was promoted driver.

In those days it was traditional for drivers to have some personal item around the engine and Jones fitted his Consolidation type locomotive with a six-tone calliope whistle. In 1900 he was transferred to Memphis to work on the crack train of the Illinois Central—the No. 1 New Orleans Special, known as "The Cannonball". He took his famous whistle with him and fitted it to the 4-6-0 locomotive no. 382.

The day which made him famous, and ended his life, was the 29th April 1900. He brought the northbound "Cannonball" in to Memphis right on time and found that the crew for the southbound working were not on duty owing to sickness. The train was already 95 minutes down and Casey and his fireman,

Sim Webb, volunteered to go right on back with it working their own engine. Jones aimed to make up 60 minutes before Grenada, another 15 minutes by Durant and be back on time at Canton. People on the line guessed that something unusual was afoot as they had only a short time earlier heard the famous whistle on the northbound train. Just south of Durant a couple of freights were switched to allow the crack express through, but the siding was short and four trucks remained on the main line. The guard of the freight which was not inside placed a detonator and ran back waving his lamp. Casey Jones, however, just could not drop from 70 miles an hour to a stand in the available distance. He ordered his fireman to jump off, but stuck to his own post and was found among the wreckage with his hand still on the air-brake handle.

He had a record of often violating the rules of the Railroad but was never involved in an accident involving loss of life and now came very near to maintaining that record as he alone died. His grandson still works on the Illinois Central and his memory lives on in the popular ballad "Casey Jones, the Brave Engineer".

Whence Pullman?

THE NAME of "Pullman" in relation to specialised railway vehicles is now a household word and derives from George Mortimer Pullman who, in 1864, put the first luxury sleeping car into service in the United States of America. The next car to be provided came in 1867 and by 1870 a complete train of these special vehicles was in service. Initially the idea was to provide decent night accommodation on the very long journeys possible in such a large country as the United States, but in time a variety of cars came into use both in America and in smaller countries with the object of giving a "hotel service" while on the move.

The first experiment with these cars in this country was on the Midland Railway in 1874 when two Pullman sleeping cars were introduced. Later the same year the Midland expanded the Pullman service to a regular train operating between London and the West Riding of Yorkshire.

Fiscal Misappropriation

A ONE-TIME City Treasurer of San Francisco absconded to Peru taking the city money with him. With this money he set up in business and, as there was no treaty in existence between the U.S.A. and Peru for dealing with such malefactors, nothing could be done to restrain him. One of the more lucrative jobs he tackled in Peru was the building of the Oraya Railway. Having done well in this commercial venture he repaid the money he had "borrowed" with interest.

A railway built with stolen money.

Pro Utilitate Hominum

THE ARGENTINE Railways used to be British owned but just after the second world war we swapped them for a great deal of frozen meat!

No Wonder – No Engine

THE FIRST steam railway in Australia was opened on the 12th September 1854 between Melbourne and Port Melbourne. The locomotive used on that day was built in Australia because those ordered from England had not arrived. However, within a few days the Australian locomotive broke down and the directors published a notice:- "The Locomotive having broken down and those from England not yet landed, the train will cease running until further notice."

The English engines arrived early in 1855.

A Miscellany

Well, Just Fancy

"BEFORE going to his engine, every engine-man should visit the notice board. After a driver has read the special notices and looked at the weekly lighting list AGAIN he proceeds to his engine. This is important for two drivers have been known to go off the same shed, chattering with each other, and when they got to the station, they found, in some strange way, that they both wanted to hook on to the same train."
(Locomotive Engine Driving: Michael Reynolds, 1878)

Dr. Lardner

FROM TIME to time one comes across the name of Dr. Dionysius Lardner in connection with railway matters. He was born in Dublin on the 3rd April 1793, the son of a solicitor. At first Lardner entered his father's business but later went to Trinity College, Dublin, and graduated there. He was appointed a professor at University College, London, in 1828, but in 1840 he eloped with a married lady and went to the United States. He later settled in Paris and became a prolific writer of popular scientific works. On the whole he was not considered an authority on railway matters but this did not prevent him from pronouncing his opinions. He died in Naples on the 29th April, 1859.

The History Of The Rail

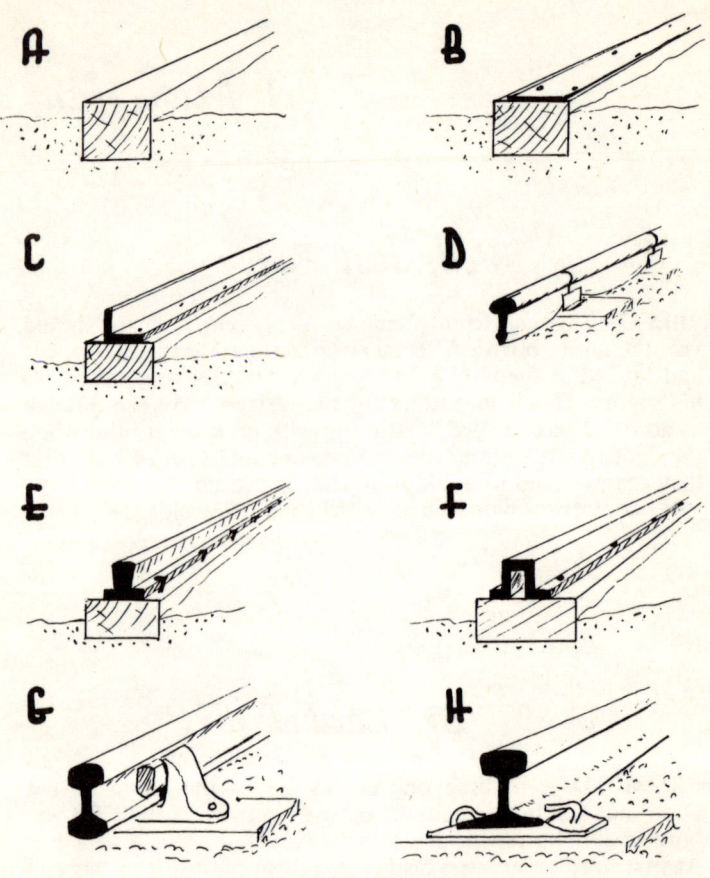

A. It was found at a very early date that waggons could more easily be hauled over smooth baulks of wood, rather than the rough stony ground.

B. As the wood wore out fairly quickly, the old waggon road owners got the idea of fastening plates of iron on to the baulks.

The men who fastened the plates down were, of course, "platelayers", a phrase which has persisted to the present day.

C.   The next problem to solve was the liability of the waggons to come off the plate-ways and so flanges were incorporated.

D.   Still later the flanges were put on the wheels and edge-rail was used, as also was a variant known as "fish-belly" rail.

E.   Because of the difficulty of rolling edge- and fish-belly rails an early form of flat-bottomed rail was invented. It had its drawbacks but could be produced more cheaply and in greater quantity than its predecessors.

F.   Popular with Mr. Brunel on the Great Western Railway was the bridge-rail.

G.   This is bull-head rail which was in common use for a very long time. It is similar to the double-headed rail invented by Joseph Locke on the Grand Junction Railway.

H.   And in modern times the railway engineers have returned to the use of flat-bottomed rail.

The Railway Clearing House

THIS institution was founded on the 2nd January 1842 as a means of allocating the receipts from through traffic between the various railway companies over whose lines it was conveyed. Previously passengers wishing to make a journey which involved travel over the lines of two or more companies had to re-book at each change. Goods also had to be transhipped from the wagons of one company to another. After the establishment of the Railway Clearing House it was possible to arrange all these journeys by one simple payment and for that payment to be then allocated in accordance with an agreed scale. Arrangements were also made for the through running of carriages and wagons of one company over the lines of others.

The first nine members of the R.C.H. were:
(1) Birmingham and Derby Junction Railway.
(2) Great North of England Railway.
(3) Hull and Selby Railway.

(4) Leeds and Selby Railway.
(5) London and Birmingham Railway.
(6) Manchester and Leeds Railway.
(7) Midland Counties Railway.
(8) North Midland Railway.
(9) York and North Midland Railway.

The Board of the R.C.H. was composed of representatives of the member companies.

What Mr. Gladstone Really Said In 1844

THE FAMOUS Gladstone Act of 9th August 1844 provided that over every line railway companies must run at least one train a day conveying third class passengers in carriages protected from the weather and at fares not exceeding one penny a mile. These trains were to stop at every station and were to be timed at a minimum speed of 12 miles an hour.

This created problems for the East Anglian Railway. It operated one of its branch lines with a horse-drawn tram which, of course, could not achieve this turn of speed!

The History Of The Signal

A. Very early on in the days of railways a primitive form of flag-signal was invented which stopped the train when standing as illustrated, and indicated "all right" when standing edgeways to the approaching train. This was invented to save the lazy railway policeman,
B, from standing out in the rain to give hand signals.
C. An improvement of the flag signal which could be seen at a greater distance. Sometimes had a white board at right-angles behind to give the all clear indication.
D. A very sophisticated signal, the revolving disc. If it stood at right-angles to the track (as illustrated) it meant a variety of things according to which quarter the open part showed. This could also be turned edgeways on to give a further indication.

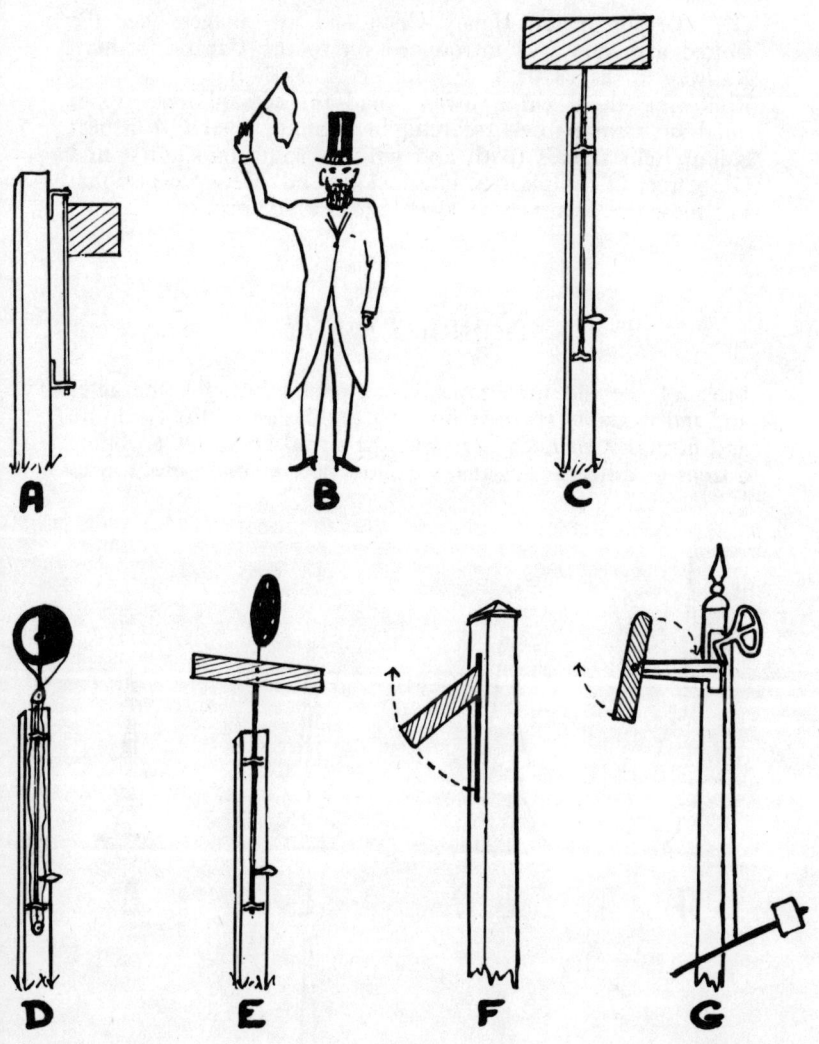

E. A disc and board signal. Nobody could ever quite remember whether the disc or the board gave the clear indication.
F. The slotted post signal which was a fairly early invention;
examples could be seen until very recently.

G. The somersault signal which had advantages over the slotted arm and was introduced on to the Great Northern Railway in the 1870s.

Following these came lower quadrant semaphores, upper quadrant semaphores, searchlight signals, 3 and 4 aspect colour light signals (with and without route indicators) and all manner of complicated interlocking and safety precautions; but these are relatively modern and are not history.

Signal Finials

Most of the old time railway companies brought character and individuality to their lines by the design of the furniture and fittings. One such item was the signal finial. Of probably dozens of different designs, we show here a small selection to

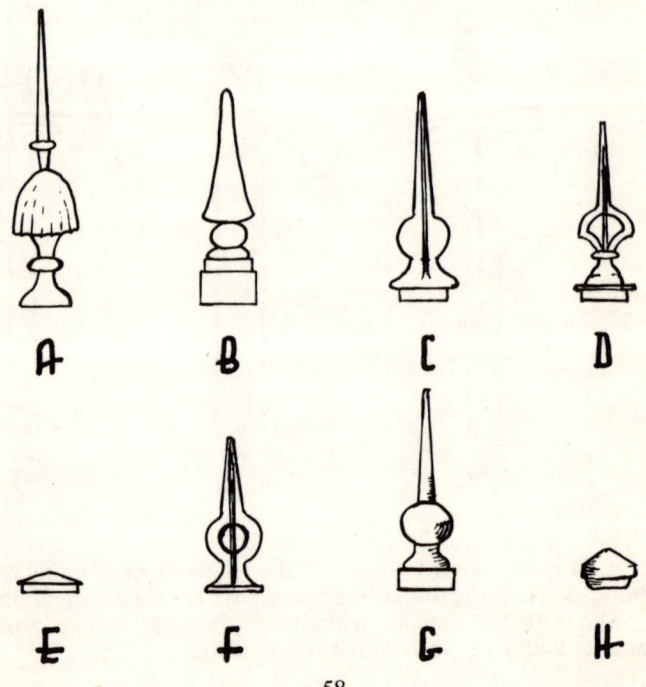

indicate the variety which could be introduced into the design of this one item.

A. North Eastern Railway.
B. Midland Railway.
C. Lancashire & Yorkshire Railway.
D. Hull & Barnsley Railway.
E. Furness Railway (among others).
F. North British Railway.
G. Great Central Railway.
H. London, Midland & Scottish Railway (tubular posts).

Sunday Funds

IN THE nineteenth century many railway directors and shareholders were strict in their desire not to benefit personally from the running of trains and the labours of men on the Sabbath. They accordingly declined to accept the proportion of dividends which derived from this source. The London and North Western Railway company paid this money into a Sunday Travelling Fund which, among other things, provided a church at Crewe.

Enough's Enough

IN THE early days of railways the carriages were smaller and lighter than we now know them. Trains therefore tended to be quite long, but in July 1854 the Superintendent of the London and North Western Railway sent out a memorandum to the effect that he thought fifty carriages was considerably more than was proper.

Well Sponsored

ROBERT Stephenson Smyth Baden Powell (the late Lord Baden-Powell, founder of the Scout Movement) was a godson of Robert Stephenson of railway fame.

To Be Treated Like Royalty

ON THE 27th December 1864 Queen Victoria wrote a letter to railway directors asking them to take as much care for the safety of her subjects as they did when she travelled by train.

Water On

WHEN constructing the railway tunnel at Ventnor in the Isle of Wight an underground spring was struck. Undismayed, the railway proprietors entered into negotiations which resulted in the water being used as the town's supply.

Water Off

WHEN Hillfield Tunnel was constructed on the South Wales Railway it was run at a depth of 200 feet under Newport. This, being lower than the wells in the town, caused them all to run dry and water had to be brought from other sources.

Present Company Always Excepted

"IT IS well known that some drivers have pulled out of a station without their trains and have not found their mistake until they overshot the next station platform, and actually then whistled for the guard to put on his brake. Others have lost eight carriages out of twelve and observed no difference in the working of the engine."
(Locomotive Engine Driving: Michael Reynolds, 1878)

Times Have Changed

BEFORE 1868 most railway companies did not permit smoking on their trains or premises but in that year Parliament made it obligatory to provide some accommodation for smokers on all trains.

No Spitting

"PLEASE do not spit in the carriages. It is offensive to other passengers and is stated by the medical profession to be a source of serious disease."
—Notice in Victorian Railway Carriages.

Railway Time

"GREENWICH time is kept at all the stations; and passengers who are as far west as Bristol should be aware that this makes a difference between the geographically local time and the railway time of nearly twelve minutes."
(The Midland Railway; Fredk. S. Williams, 1877)

Edible Passengers

"GENTLEMEN having seats in the country, and residing occasionally in London, may have fruit and vegetables for their own use conveyed from any station in the country by passenger train and delivered in London at reduced rates."
(The Midland Railway; Fredk. S. Williams, 1877)

Highest

THE GREATEST altitude reached by a railway is 15,848 feet above sea level on the Peruvian Central Railway. This is a standard gauge line. Greatest altitude in Great Britain—Snowden Mountain Railway, 3,540 feet, 2ft. 7½ins. gauge. Highest standard gauge, main-line—Druimuachdar Summit, 1,484 feet.

Longest

SIMPLON Tunnel, opened in 1921, is 12 miles 559 yards long. The longest tunnel in the British Isles (and indeed in the world) is actually the $17\frac{1}{4}$ mile tube railway between Morden and East Finchley but the longest conventional tunnel is the Severn—4 miles 629 yards.

The Great Coat Fiasco

AT THE END of the great war the army authorities decided that demobbed soldiers could keep their uniforms except for the greatcoat and for this they were to be paid a pound.

But this little transaction was not carried out at the place of demobilisation. To make it easier for the retired Tommies, the Government asked the railways to take in the coats at any station and to pay out the pounds. The Post Office had refused the job and the railways wished that they had refused it too.

Step Aside While I Pass

SIR JOHN Aspinall in an address to the Institute of Mechanical Engineers in 1925 recalled a practice which he knew in his early years on the London and North Western Railway. At a place where the leading engine of a double-headed train was to be detached, the fireman had to clamber over the tender and unhook the coupling. The engine then put on speed in order to get ahead and be able to reverse into a siding to let the train pass...

All this seems to have demanded a clear head and quick action by the train crew and by the signalman who switched the points. It recalls to mind a form of "snatch-shunting" which I knew as a boy around the G.W.R. goods yards at Saltney, near Chester. The pannier tank engine and a few wagons would come along the line and at a certain point one shunter would unhook the last wagon. The engine and remainder then would shoot off at great speed while a second shunter would throw the points after it to allow the detached wagon to run into another siding under its own momentum. It certainly avoided running the engine round the rake and it was always carried out accurately.

Railway Saints

1. Saint Pancras was a Phrygian who went with his uncle to Rome where he was beheaded in 286 A.D. for being a Christian.

2. Saint Rollox (a Scottish variation of the name Saint Roch) was a native of Montpellier in France. He is regarded as the protector against pestilence and plagues and lived from 1295 to 1327.

3. Saint Enoch (otherwise known as Saint Kennocha) was a Scottish nun who lived in a convent in Fife and was well-known in the Glasgow area. She died in 1007.

—St. Pancras

On The Straight

WORLD RECORD for a dead straight run of railway track is across the Nullarbor Desert in Australia. This is 328 miles long. The longest straight line in Britain occurs between Selby and Hull—18 miles.

Blow You, Jack

AT THE meeting of the Railway Clerks' Association held on the 25th May 1927, a delegate representing the clerks in the passenger departments pointed out the odd hours which they were required to work. He stated, "On Bank Holidays our friends, the goods clerks, on their way to Ilkley Moor or Margate, poke their heads into the office and say 'Are you on duty?'. We don't mind that, but when on their return they ask us if we have had a nice day, it is too much."

High Speed Rail

THE PROBLEMS of high speed on railways are not so much connected with providing adequate motive power as with achieving sufficient stability for the train. In 1930 a German inventor fitted an air screw propeller to a passenger carriage and ran this at over 140 miles an hour on a dead straight track. This was followed in this country by a type of mono-rail system which was erected near Glasgow.

Again air screw propellers were used, but the fully stream-lined carriage was suspended from a single rail and equipped with stabilising wheels running against a rail below the car. By this means curves could be taken quite safely at speed. Adhesive weight is not required for this form of propulsion so the vehicles can be so much lighter and the rail resistance very low. Gradients up to about 1 in 27 are tolerable.

High Speed Trains

THE RECORD speed for steam traction was achieved by the L.N.E.R. engine *Mallard* on 3rd July 1938 when it reached 126 m.p.h. at one point and, over a five-mile stretch, averaged 120.4 m.p.h. In France a train powered by turbojet aircraft engines reached 235 m.p.h. in 1967.

Warning To Students

THE STUDENT of railway history should never lose sight of the political situation surrounding his subject (using the word political in its broadest sense).

For instance, he should remember that, even after steam traction had been invented for many years the vested interests of the stage coach fraternity effectively checked its widespread introduction on the roads. The historical facts of political life have repercussions over the whole national scene and we see that after the Napoleonic Wars, which Britain did not get out of until Waterloo (the battle, not the railway station), there was a grave shortage of horses. This gave an added stimulus to alternative methods of traction and as the roads had lost their chance the railways stepped in and were quickly developed.

It is interesting to speculate whether or not we should have had an excellent system of roads and no railways if events had gone otherwise. No Beeching and lots of motorways!

The Welfare Of Railway Workers

OVER A period of about 150 years there have been in existence many hundreds of railway companies, some quite small and some very large. In the heyday of the railways they employed a substantial percentage of the nation's population, and it is hardly surprising that the railway companies (or such of them as were large enough) and the men themselves gave serious thought to the problem of providing for the welfare of the railway worker and his family.

Many of the organisations which have been founded over this period are still in existence, although altered circumstances in the modern welfare state have in some cases modified their original purposes. Some of the pre-Grouping companies had (for those days) quite good superannuation or pension schemes and these have been taken over by their successors. Men are still receiving allowances in supplementation of their state pensions from these sources.

Some of the voluntary organisations which are still in being were founded for the purpose of improving the morals of the employees as well as for providing benefits in time of sickness, unemployment or retirement. Among these organisations may be named:

Railway Benevolent Institution.   Founded 1858.

Financial relief for members who are permanently incapacitated and for their widows and orphans. Runs a home for aged retired railwaymen and their widows. Has a life Assurance branch and an accident fund.

Railway Convalescent Homes.

In common with many of the larger industries the railways have, from an early date, provided convalescent homes at various seaside centres for the recuperation of their members and families.

The Railway Mission.   Founded 1882.

Even before the founding of the Mission there had been a good deal of Christian work carried on in canteens and waiting rooms with the permission of the railway companies. This was particularly welcome in an era of greater Christian awareness than we are used to finding today, and in what was then one of the very few industries in which men were required to work on Sundays and were thus kept away from their normal places of worship.

The Mission once had over 400 centres but now has only 50. Two of the railway convalescent homes were established by the Railway Mission.

Railway Officers' & Servants' Association.   Founded 1861.

Helps needy railwaymen, their widows and orphans. In the past 100 years has paid out over £600,000 to those in distressed circumstances. Has a sick fund which supplements state benefits in time of illness.

British Railways Temperance Union.
Founded in 1882 as the United Kingdom Railway Temperance Union, this organisation was promoted by the Church of England Temperance Union with the following objects:
1. The promotion of total abstinence from alcoholic liquor among railwaymen, their wives and children.
2. The reformation of the intemperate.
3. The removal of causes which lead to intemperance. The Union published a magazine *On The Line* continuously from January 1883 to September 1961. Most of the old railway companies encouraged their men to form temperance and abstinence societies and these were affiliated to the U.K.R.T.U.

Interesting Points Of Biography

Arroll, Sir William. 13 February 1839 – 20 February 1913.
Originally worked in a cotton mill, then became a blacksmith. Later he became an expert in construction in steel and built the Tay, Forth and Tower Bridges as well as being engaged in the construction of the Manchester Ship Canal.

Brunel, Isambard Kingdom. 9 April 1806 – 15 September 1859.
Of French extraction. Became engineer to the Great Western Railway at the early age of 27. Was also interested in ocean steam navigation. Was an enthusiastic worker for the Great Exhibition of 1851. Designed guns and hospitals for the war against Russia 1854. He was a heavy smoker and carried a large leather case which held 50 cigars.

Cook, Thomas. 22 November 1808 – 19 July 1892.
A native of Derbyshire, he ran the first advertised excursion on 5th July 1841 on the Midland Counties Railway. Had been a Baptist preacher and missionary. Founded the well-known world wide travel agency of Thomas Cook and Son.

Caprotti, Arturo. 1882 – 1938.
An Italian engineer who invented the rotary camshaft valve gear which bears his name.

Churchward, G. J. 1857 – 1933.
This famous locomotive engineer of the Great Western

Railway was killed instantly on the morning of 19th December 1933 when struck by an express train on the main line at Swindon.

Edmondson, Thomas.   1792 – 22 June 1851.

Before becoming stationmaster on the Newcastle and Carlisle Railway he had been a grocer and a cabinet maker. He invented and perfected his pasteboard tickets and his dating machines over a period. Later went to the Manchester and Leeds Railway. He fixed the size of the ticket which is still used, viz: 2¼ins. x 1$\frac{3}{16}$ins.

Ericcson, John.   31 July 1803 – 8 March 1889.

Born in Sweden. Started work as a draughtsman at the age of 12. A prolific inventor. Came to England in 1826 and, with John Braithwaite, constructed a locomotive which they entered in the Rainhill trials. Went to U.S.A. in 1839, becoming naturalised and staying there until his death. He was buried in Sweden 18 months after he died.

Hudson, George.   March 1800 – 14 December 1871.

A linen draper of York. Spent as much as £3,000 a day in legal fees to fight other railways. Three times Lord Mayor of York. Was a Member of Parliament from 1845 to 1859.

Huish, Captain Mark.

Used the title of "Captain" on the strength of having held that rank in the Indian Army as a very young man. Originally with the Grand Junction Railway, then General Manager to the London and North Western Railway.

Stephens, Lt. Col. Holman F., M.I.C.E.

A happy man! In boyhood he had a model railway layout and in manhood he was General Manager/Engineer/Locomotive Superintendent/Managing Director/etc. to any number of small light railways.

Stephenson, George.   9 June 1781 – 12 August 1848.

Learnt to read when he was 18. First successful trial with a steam locomotive 25 July 1814.

Stephenson, Robert.   16 October 1803 – 12 October 1859.

Perfected the tube boiler. Was a mining engineer in South America from 1824 to 1827. Became a Member of Parliament in 1847. Is buried in Westminster Abbey.

Trevithick, Richard. 13 April 1771 – 22 April 1833.
Stood 6ft. 2 ins. high. Successfully hauled passengers in a
steam road vehicle on 24 December 1801. First steam railway
locomotive February 1804.

Vanderbilt, Cornelius. 27 May 1794 – 1877.
Founded the fortunes of this wealthy American family by
buying a boat when he was 16 and ferrying passengers and
goods from Staten Island to New York. In 1857 he got out of
shipping and went in for railroad speculating.

Walschaerts, Egide. 1820 – 1901.
A Belgian railway mechanic who invented his famous valve
gear in 1844.

Westinghouse, George. 6 October 1846 – 12 March 1914.
An American engineer who built the dynamoes for Niagara
Falls Generating Station. Invented the compressed air brake
in 1865 and developed railway signalling.

Notable Firsts

First Pullman carriage in England—Midland Railway 25th
January 1874.

First train of complete stock in which it was possible to walk
from end to end of the train, with lavatories available to all
classes and carriage warming throughout—London to
Bradford service of the Midland Railway, 1st June 1874.

First large organised excursion—Midland Counties Railway
when Nottingham Mechanics' Institute members visited
Leicester on the 20th July 1840.

First modern type railway tickets invented by Edmondson were
used on the Birmingham and Gloucester Railway.

First use of semaphore signalling on railways—London and
Croydon Railway 1841 or 1842.

First season tickets—Canterbury and Whitstable Rly. 1834.

First installation of automatic signalling on a steam railway in this country was between Andover Junction and Grateley on the 31st July 1901. Pneumatic operation of points at Grateley followed on 20th April 1902.

First bolted fishplates—Eastern Counties Railway 1849. Engineer: J. Samuel.

First slip coaches—London, Brighton and South Coast Railway. Slipped at Haywards Heath on 1st February 1858.

First fishtail distant signal—London, Brighton and South Coast Railway, Norwood Junction. August 1872.

First electric lighting of railway carriages—Pullman car on the London. Brighton and South Coast Railway on 14th October 1881. Fed by accumulators charged at Victoria.

First trip by a reigning monarch on a railway—Great Western Railway, 13th June 1842, Next royal trip was on the London and Southampton Railway in 1843.

First signalbox in the world was on the London and Greenwich Railway.

First train ferry—Edinburgh, Perth and Dundee Railway, opened 7th February 1850 with the paddle steamer *Leviathan*. Crossed the Firth of Forth.

First railway tunnel in the world—Bullo Pill Railway (Gloucestershire). 1,100 yards long. Built 1810.

First tunnel to be used by passenger trains—Canterbury and Whitstable Railway 1830.

First steam heating of passenger carriages—Caledonian Railway, April 1883.

First coal by rail to London—Midland Railway, 1845. Taken from the North, via Rugby and the London and North Western line.

First public railway in the world to carry fare-paying passengers—Oystermouth Railway, 25th March 1807.

70

First mails by railway—Grand Junction Railway, 4th July 1837.

First Travelling Post Office—Grand Junction Railway. Ran between Liverpool and Birmingham, 6th January 1838.

First railway to operate under a public Act of Parliament—Surrey Iron Railway, 1801.

First railway built under a Light Railway Order—Basingstoke and Alton Light Railway, 1897.

First fatal accident involving a railway locomotive—Liverpool and Manchester Railway, 30th September 1834. Mr. Huskisson, the Home Secretary, was killed.

First issue of signal diagrams, etc., to drivers—London, and South Western Railway, about 1869.

First telegraph installed on a railway in 1841 giving communication between either end of Clay Cross tunnel on the Midland Railway.

First underground railway in the world—Metropolitan Railway London.

First "fly-over" junction—Weaver Junction, London and North Western Railway, 1869. Up Liverpool line crossed over both roads of the Carlisle line.

First water troughs—Mochdre, near Llandudno Junction, London and North Western Railway, 1860.

First strike of railway workers—Liverpool and Manchester Railway, February 1836.

First sleeping carriage—North British Railway, April 1873.

First meals cooked and eaten on a train, 1879.

Can't You Sleep?

THIS IS a bedside book and I hope it has lulled you to a peaceful slumber on more than one occasion, but if all else fails try this.

Imagine yourself standing on a railway platform near to a steam engine with a small boy beside you. Now you must describe the workings of a steam locomotive so that the boy may understand just how it is. You are not permitted to wave your arms about although you may point to the particular part of the locomotive which you are describing.